Home Education DIARY

The comprehensive undated planner for home educators to plan and record the academic year in a personalised manner.

Name

Date

Home Education Diary

CONTENTS:

Goals and objectives

Year overview

June

July

August

Topic overview

June

July

August

Internet resources

Resource:
Password:
Additional notes:

Password
Additional notes:

Learning trips and visits

Place visited:
What we have learnt:

Place visited:
What we have learnt:

Place visited:
What we

Contacts

Contact	Details

Daily Plans

Mon

Tues

Wed

Thurs

Learning achieved

Subject	Achievements

Personal record of things I've learnt

Things I've learnt

Subject	

Notes:

Personal overview of week

What I enjoyed most:

How can I use what I've learnt:

Additional notes:

Goals and objectives

Goals and objectives

Goals and objectives

Goals and objectives

Year overview

June

July

August

Year overview

September

_____

_____

_____

_____

October

_____

_____

_____

November

_____

_____

_____

_____

Year overview

December

January

February

March

_____

- -

- -

- -

April

- -

- -

- -

- -

May

_____

- -

- -

- -

Year overview

June

July

August

Notes

Topic overview

June

_____

_____

_____

_____

July

_____

_____

_____

_____

August

_____

_____

_____

_____

Topic overview

September

October

November

Topic overview

December

January

February

Topic overview

March

April

May

Topic overview

June

July

August

Notes

Reading log

Title:_____

Author:_____

Comments:_____

_____

_____

Title:_____

Author:_____

Comments:_____

_____

_____

Title:_____

Author:_____

Comments:_____

_____

_____

Reading log

Title:_____

Author:_____

Comments:_____

_____

_____

Title:_____

Author:_____

Comments:_____

_____

_____

Title:_____

Author:_____

Comments:_____

_____

_____

Reading log

Title:_____

Author:_____

Comments:_____

_____

_____

Title:_____

Author:_____

Comments:_____

_____

_____

Title:_____

Author:_____

Comments:_____

_____

_____

Reading log

Title:_____

Author:_____

Comments:_____

_____

_____

Title:_____

Author:_____

Comments:_____

_____

_____

Title:_____

Author:_____

Comments:_____

_____

_____

Reading log

Title:_____

Author:_____

Comments:_____

_____

_____

Title:_____

Author:_____

Comments:_____

_____

_____

Title:_____

Author:_____

Comments:_____

_____

_____

Reading log

Title:_____

Author:_____

Comments:_____

_____

_____

Title:_____

Author:_____

Comments:_____

_____

_____

Title:_____

Author:_____

Comments:_____

_____

_____

Reading log

Title:_____

Author:_____

Comments:_____

_____

_____

Title:_____

Author:_____

Comments:_____

_____

_____

Title:_____

Author:_____

Comments:_____

_____

_____

Reading log

Title:_____

Author:_____

Comments:_____

_____

_____

Title:_____

Author:_____

Comments:_____

_____

_____

Title:_____

Author:_____

Comments:_____

_____

_____

Reading log

Title:_____

Author:_____

Comments:_____

_____

_____

Title:_____

Author:_____

Comments:_____

_____

_____

Title:_____

Author:_____

Comments:_____

_____

_____

Reading log

Title:_____

Author:_____

Comments:_____

_____

_____

Title:_____

Author:_____

Comments:_____

_____

_____

Title:_____

Author:_____

Comments:_____

_____

_____

Reading log

Title:_____

Author:_____

Comments:_____

_____

_____

Title:_____

Author:_____

Comments:_____

_____

_____

Title:_____

Author:_____

Comments:_____

_____

_____

Notes

Internet resources

Resource:

_____

Password:

Additional notes:

Password:

Additional notes:

Resource:

Password:

Additional notes:

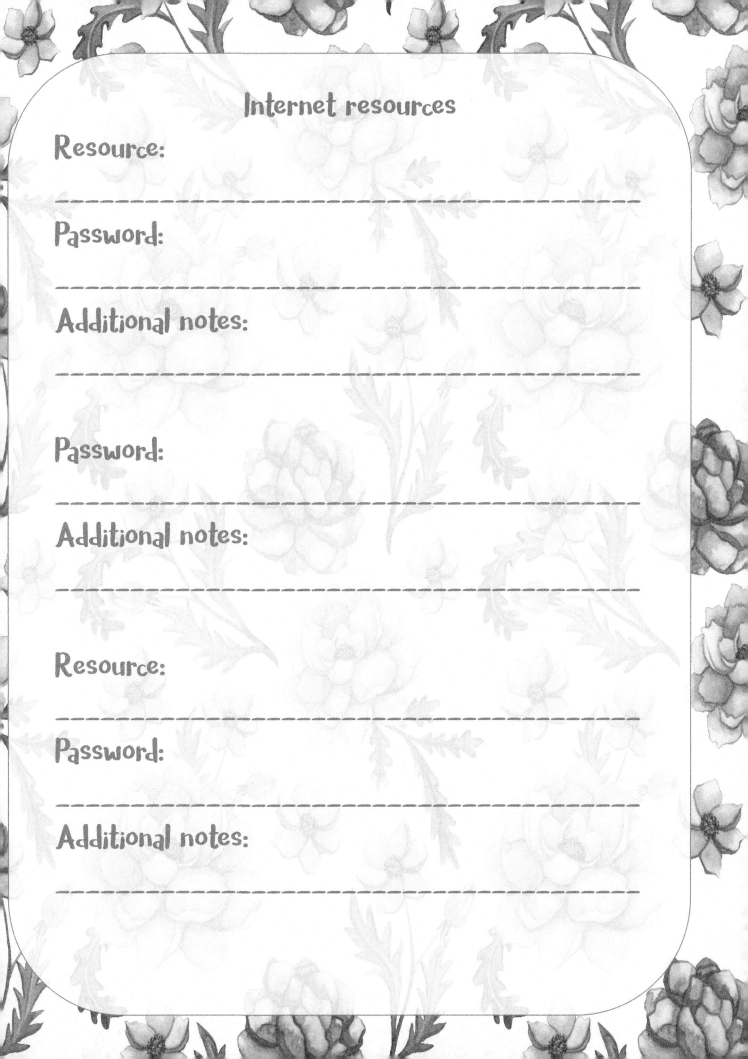

Internet resources

Resource:

Password:

Additional notes:

Password:

Additional notes:

Resource:

Password:

Additional notes:

Internet resources

Resource:

_____

Password:

_____

Additional notes:

_____

Password:

_____

Additional notes:

_____

Resource:

_____

Password:

_____

Additional notes:

_____

Internet resources

Resource:

Password:

Additional notes:

Password:

Additional notes:

Resource:

Password:

Additional notes:

Internet resources

Resource:

_____

Password:

_____

Additional notes:

_____

Password:

_____

Additional notes:

_____

Resource:

_____

Password:

_____

Additional notes:

_____

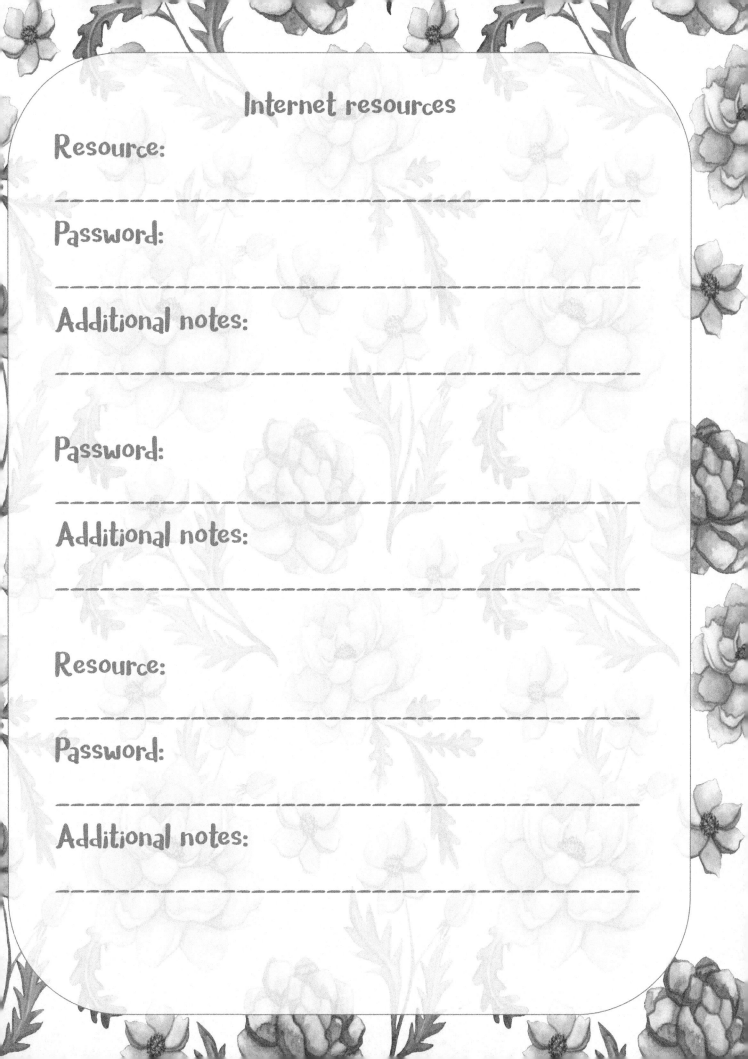

Internet resources

Resource:

Password:

Additional notes:

Password:

Additional notes:

Resource:

Password:

Additional notes:

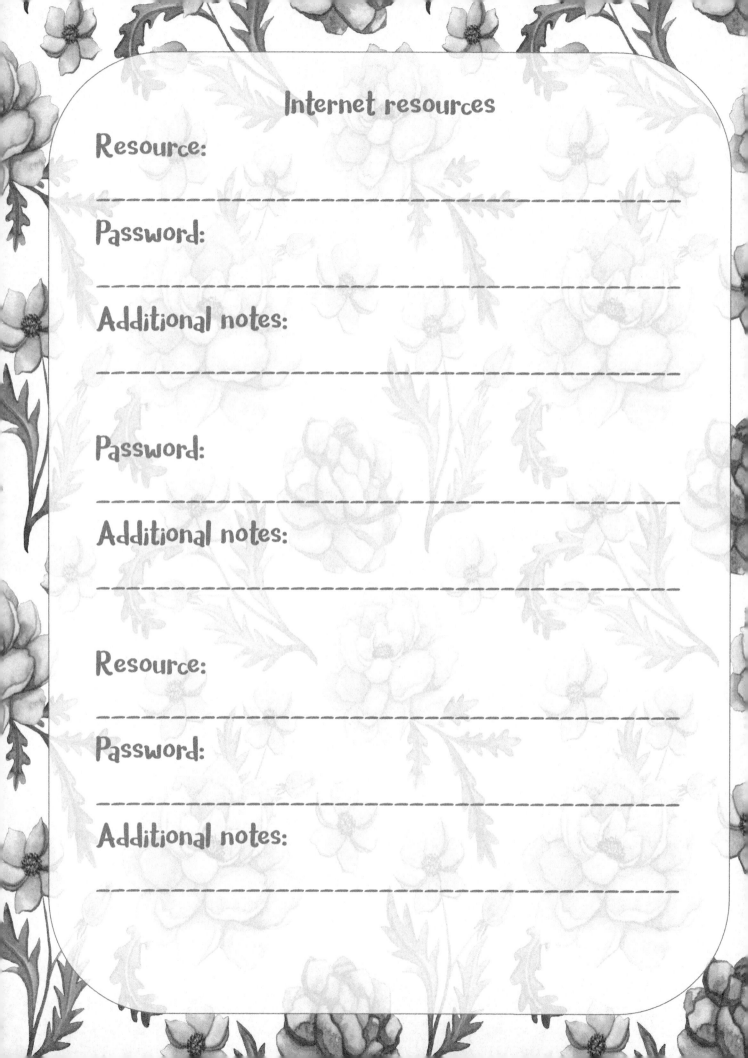

Internet resources

Resource:

_____

Password:

_____

Additional notes:

_____

Password:

_____

Additional notes:

_____

Resource:

_____

Password:

_____

Additional notes:

_____

Internet resources

Resource:

Password:

Additional notes:

Password:

Additional notes:

Resource:

Password:

Additional notes:

Notes

Notes

Learning trips and visits

Place visited:

What we have learnt:

Place visited:

What we have learnt:

Place visited:

What we have learnt:

Learning trips and visits

Place visited:

What we have learnt:

Place visited:

What we have learnt:

Place visited:

What we have learnt:

Learning trips and visits

Place visited:

_____

What we have learnt:

_____

_____

_____

Place visited:

_____

What we have learnt:

_____

_____

_____

Place visited:

_____

What we have learnt:

_____

_____

_____

Learning trips and visits

Place visited:

_____

What we have learnt:

_____

_____

_____

Place visited:

_____

What we have learnt:

_____

_____

_____

Place visited:

_____

What we have learnt:

_____

_____

_____

Learning trips and visits

Place visited:

_____

What we have learnt:

_____

_____

_____

Place visited:

_____

What we have learnt:

_____

_____

_____

Place visited:

_____

What we have learnt:

_____

_____

_____

Notes

Notes

Notes

Daily Plans

Mon				
Tues				
Wed				
Thurs				
Fri				

Learning achieved

Subject	Achievements

Personal record of things I've learnt

Subject	Things I've learnt

Personal overview of week

What I enjoyed most:

_____

_____

_____

How can I use what I've learnt:

_____

_____

_____

Additional notes:

Daily Plans

Mon				
Tues				
Wed				
Thurs				
Fri				

Learning achieved

Subject	Achievements

Personal record of things I've learnt

Subject	Things I've learnt

Personal overview of week

What I enjoyed most:

_____

_____

_____

How can I use what I've learnt:

_____

_____

_____

Additional notes:

Daily Plans

Mon				
Tues				
Wed				
Thurs				
Fri				

Learning achieved

Subject	Achievements

Personal record of things I've learnt

Subject	Things I've learnt

Personal overview of week

What I enjoyed most:

_____

_____

_____

How can I use what I've learnt:

_____

_____

_____

Additional notes:

Daily Plans

Mon				
Tues				
Wed				
Thurs				
Fri				

Learning achieved

Subject	Achievements

Personal record of things I've learnt

Subject	Things I've learnt

Personal overview of week

What I enjoyed most:

_____

_____

_____

How can I use what I've learnt:

_____

_____

_____

Additional notes:

Daily Plans

Mon				
Tues				
Wed				
Thurs				
Fri				

Learning achieved

Subject	Achievements

Personal record of things I've learnt

Subject	Things I've learnt

Personal overview of week

What I enjoyed most:

_____

_____

_____

How can I use what I've learnt:

_____

_____

_____

Additional notes:

Daily Plans

Mon				
Tues				
Wed				
Thurs				
Fri				

Learning achieved

Subject	Achievements

Personal record of things I've learnt

Subject	Things I've learnt

Personal overview of week

What I enjoyed most:

_____

_____

_____

How can I use what I've learnt:

_____

_____

_____

Additional notes:

Daily Plans

Mon				
Tues				
Wed				
Thurs				
Fri				

Learning achieved

Subject	Achievements

Personal record of things I've learnt

Subject	Things I've learnt

Personal overview of week

What I enjoyed most:

_____

_____

_____

How can I use what I've learnt:

_____

_____

_____

Additional notes:

Daily Plans

Mon				
Tues				
Wed				
Thurs				
Fri				

Learning achieved

Subject	Achievements

Personal record of things I've learnt

Subject	Things I've learnt

Personal overview of week

What I enjoyed most:

_____

_____

_____

How can I use what I've learnt:

_____

_____

_____

Additional notes:

Daily Plans

Mon				
Tues				
Wed				
Thurs				
Fri				

Learning achieved

Subject	Achievements

Personal record of things I've learnt

Subject	Things I've learnt

Personal overview of week

What I enjoyed most:

_____

_____

_____

How can I use what I've learnt:

_____

_____

_____

Additional notes:

Daily Plans

Mon				
Tues				
Wed				
Thurs				
Fri				

Learning achieved

Subject	Achievements

Personal record of things I've learnt

Subject	Things I've learnt

Personal overview of week

What I enjoyed most:

_____

_____

_____

How can I use what I've learnt:

_____

_____

_____

Additional notes:

Daily Plans

Mon				
Tues				
Wed				
Thurs				
Fri				

Learning achieved

Subject	Achievements

Personal record of things I've learnt

Subject	Things I've learnt

Personal overview of week

What I enjoyed most:

_____

_____

_____

How can I use what I've learnt:

_____

_____

_____

Additional notes:

Daily Plans

Mon				
Tues				
Wed				
Thurs				
Fri				

Learning achieved

Subject	Achievements

Personal record of things I've learnt

Subject	Things I've learnt

Personal overview of week

What I enjoyed most:

_____

_____

_____

How can I use what I've learnt:

_____

_____

_____

Additional notes:

Daily Plans

Mon				
Tues				
Wed				
Thurs				
Fri				

Learning achieved

Subject	Achievements

Personal record of things I've learnt

Subject	Things I've learnt

Personal overview of week

What I enjoyed most:

_____

_____

_____

How can I use what I've learnt:

_____

_____

_____

Additional notes:

Daily Plans

Mon.				
Tues				
Wed				
Thurs				
Fri				

Learning achieved

Subject	Achievements

Personal record of things I've learnt

Subject	Things I've learnt

Personal overview of week

What I enjoyed most:

_____

_____

_____

How can I use what I've learnt:

_____

_____

_____

Additional notes:

Daily Plans

Mon				
Tues				
Wed				
Thurs				
Fri				

Learning achieved

Subject	Achievements

Personal record of things I've learnt

Subject	Things I've learnt

Personal overview of week

What I enjoyed most:

_____

_____

_____

How can I use what I've learnt:

_____

_____

_____

Additional notes:

Daily Plans

Mon				
Tues				
Wed				
Thurs				
Fri				

Learning achieved

Subject	Achievements

Personal record of things I've learnt

Subject	Things I've learnt

Personal overview of week

What I enjoyed most:

_____

_____

_____

How can I use what I've learnt:

_____

_____

_____

Additional notes:

Daily Plans

Mon				
Tues				
Wed				
Thurs				
Fri				

Learning achieved

Subject	Achievements

Personal record of things I've learnt

Subject	Things I've learnt

Personal overview of week

What I enjoyed most:

_____

_____

_____

How can I use what I've learnt:

_____

_____

_____

Additional notes:

Daily Plans

Mon				
Tues				
Wed				
Thurs				
Fri				

Learning achieved

Subject	Achievements

Personal record of things I've learnt

Subject	Things I've learnt

Personal overview of week

What I enjoyed most:

_____

_____

_____

How can I use what I've learnt:

_____

_____

_____

Additional notes:

Daily Plans

Mon				
Tues				
Wed				
Thurs				
Fri				

Learning achieved

Subject	Achievements

Personal record of things I've learnt

Subject	Things I've learnt

Personal overview of week

What I enjoyed most:

_____

_____

_____

How can I use what I've learnt:

_____

_____

_____

Additional notes:

Daily Plans

Mon				
Tues				
Wed				
Thurs				
Fri				

Learning achieved

Subject	Achievements

Personal record of things I've learnt

Subject	Things I've learnt

Personal overview of week

What I enjoyed most:

_____

_____

_____

How can I use what I've learnt:

_____

_____

_____

Additional notes:

Daily Plans

Mon				
Tues				
Wed				
Thurs				
Fri				

Learning achieved

Subject	Achievements

Personal record of things I've learnt

Subject	Things I've learnt

Personal overview of week

What I enjoyed most:

_____

_____

_____

How can I use what I've learnt:

_____

_____

_____

Additional notes:

Daily Plans

Mon				
Tues				
Wed				
Thurs				
Fri				

Learning achieved

Subject	Achievements

Personal record of things I've learnt

Subject	Things I've learnt

Personal overview of week

What I enjoyed most:

_____

_____

_____

How can I use what I've learnt:

_____

_____

_____

Additional notes:

Daily Plans

Mon				
Tues				
Wed				
Thurs				
Fri				

Learning achieved

Subject	Achievements

Personal record of things I've learnt

Subject	Things I've learnt

Personal overview of week

What I enjoyed most:

_____

_____

_____

How can I use what I've learnt:

_____

_____

_____

Additional notes:

Daily Plans

Mon				
Tues				
Wed				
Thurs				
Fri				

Learning achieved

Subject	Achievements

Personal record of things I've learnt

Subject	Things I've learnt

Personal overview of week

What I enjoyed most:

_____

_____

_____

How can I use what I've learnt:

_____

_____

_____

Additional notes:

Daily Plans

Mon				
Tues				
Wed				
Thurs				
Fri				

Learning achieved

Subject	Achievements

Personal record of things I've learnt

Subject	Things I've learnt

Personal overview of week

What I enjoyed most:

_____

_____

_____

How can I use what I've learnt:

_____

_____

_____

Additional notes:

Daily Plans

Mon				
Tues				
Wed				
Thurs				
Fri				

Learning achieved

Subject	Achievements

Personal record of things I've learnt

Subject	Things I've learnt

Personal overview of week

What I enjoyed most:

_____

_____

_____

How can I use what I've learnt:

_____

_____

_____

Additional notes:

Daily Plans

Mon				
Tues				
Wed				
Thurs				
Fri				

Learning achieved

Subject	Achievements

Personal record of things I've learnt

Subject	Things I've learnt

Personal overview of week

What I enjoyed most:

_____

_____

_____

How can I use what I've learnt:

_____

_____

_____

Additional notes:

Daily Plans

Mon				
Tues				
Wed				
Thurs				
Fri				

Learning achieved

Subject	Achievements

Personal record of things I've learnt

Subject	Things I've learnt

Personal overview of week

What I enjoyed most:

_____

_____

_____

How can I use what I've learnt:

_____

_____

_____

Additional notes:

Daily Plans

Mon				
Tues				
Wed				
Thurs				
Fri				

Learning achieved

Subject	Achievements

Personal record of things I've learnt

Subject	Things I've learnt

Personal overview of week

What I enjoyed most:

_____

_____

_____

How can I use what I've learnt:

_____

_____

_____

Additional notes:

Daily Plans

Mon				
Tues				
Wed				
Thurs				
Fri				

Learning achieved

Subject	Achievements

Personal record of things I've learnt

Subject	Things I've learnt

Personal overview of week

What I enjoyed most:

How can I use what I've learnt:

Additional notes:

Daily Plans

Mon				
Tues				
Wed				
Thurs				
Fri				

Learning achieved

Subject	Achievements

Personal record of things I've learnt

Subject	Things I've learnt

Personal overview of week

What I enjoyed most:

_____

_____

_____

How can I use what I've learnt:

_____

_____

_____

Additional notes:

Daily Plans

Mon				
Tues				
Wed				
Thurs				
Fri				

Learning achieved

Subject	Achievements

Personal record of things I've learnt

Subject	Things I've learnt

Personal overview of week

What I enjoyed most:

_____

_____

_____

How can I use what I've learnt:

_____

_____

_____

Additional notes:

Daily Plans

Mon				
Tues				
Wed				
Thurs				
Fri				

Learning achieved

Subject	Achievements

Personal record of things I've learnt

Subject	Things I've learnt

Personal overview of week

What I enjoyed most:

_____

_____

_____

How can I use what I've learnt:

_____

_____

_____

Additional notes:

Daily Plans

Mon				
Tues				
Wed				
Thurs				
Fri				

Learning achieved

Subject	Achievements

Personal record of things I've learnt

Subject	Things I've learnt

Personal overview of week

What I enjoyed most:

_____

_____

_____

How can I use what I've learnt:

_____

_____

_____

Additional notes:

Daily Plans

Mon				
Tues				
Wed				
Thurs				
Fri				

Learning achieved

Subject	Achievements

Personal record of things I've learnt

Subject	Things I've learnt

Personal overview of week

What I enjoyed most:

_____

_____

_____

How can I use what I've learnt:

_____

_____

_____

Additional notes:

Daily Plans

Mon				
Tues				
Wed				
Thurs				
Fri				

Learning achieved

Subject	Achievements

Personal record of things I've learnt

Subject	Things I've learnt

Personal overview of week

What I enjoyed most:

_____

_____

_____

How can I use what I've learnt:

_____

_____

_____

Additional notes:

Daily Plans

Mon				
Tues				
Wed				
Thurs				
Fri				

Learning achieved

Subject	Achievements

Personal record of things I've learnt

Subject	Things I've learnt

Personal overview of week

What I enjoyed most:

_____

_____

_____

How can I use what I've learnt:

_____

_____

_____

Additional notes:

Daily Plans

Mon				
Tues				
Wed				
Thurs				
Fri				

Learning achieved

Subject	Achievements

Personal record of things I've learnt

Subject	Things I've learnt

Personal overview of week

What I enjoyed most:

_____

_____

_____

How can I use what I've learnt:

_____

_____

_____

Additional notes:

Daily Plans

Mon				
Tues				
Wed				
Thurs				
Fri				

Learning achieved

Subject	Achievements

Personal record of things I've learnt

Subject	Things I've learnt

Personal overview of week

What I enjoyed most:

_____

_____

_____

How can I use what I've learnt:

_____

_____

_____

Additional notes:

Daily Plans

Mon				
Tues				
Wed				
Thurs				
Fri				

Learning achieved

Subject	Achievements

Personal record of things I've learnt

Subject	Things I've learnt

Personal overview of week

What I enjoyed most:

_____

_____

_____

How can I use what I've learnt:

_____

_____

_____

Additional notes:

Notes

Notes

Contacts

Contact	Details

Contacts

Contact	Details

Contacts

Contact	Details

Contacts

Contact	Details

Contacts

Contact	Details

Contacts

Contact	Details

Contacts

Contact	Details

Contacts

Contact	Details

Notes:

Notes:

Notes:

Notes:

Notes:

Notes

Printed in Great Britain
by Amazon

39431843R00126